Companion Planting:

The Vegetable Gardeners Guide To

The Role of Flowers, Herbs & Organic Thinking

By

James Paris

Published By

www.deanburnpublications.com

Blog: www.planterspost.com

2nd Edition Update January 2015
ISBN-10: 1499635095
ISBN-13: 978-1499635096

Relevant Books by Same Author

Raised Bed Gardening 5 Book Bundle
Square Foot Gardening
Square Foot Vs Raised Bed Gardening
Vegetable Gardening Basics
Organic Pest Control

James Paris is an **Amazon Best Selling Author**, you can see the full range of books on his Amazon author page.

http://amazon.com/author/jamesparis

Copyright:

Copyright © 2014-20, James Paris

All rights reserved. Copyright protected. Duplicating, reprinting or distributing this material without the express written consent of the author is prohibited.

While reasonable attempts have been made to assure the accuracy of the information contained within this publication, the author does not assume any responsibility for errors, omissions or contrary interpretation of this information, and any damages incurred by that.

The author does not assume any responsibility or liability whatsoever, for what you choose to do with this information.

Table of Contents

Introduction to Companion Planting Vegetables: 5
The History of Companion Planting: 8
    Planting Zones: 10
5 Good Reasons For Companion Planting: 14
The influence of Allelopathy: 18
Why Plants Grow Well Together: 21
Plants That Grow Well Together: 24
Plants That Do Not Grow Well Together: 30
Quick Reference Companion Planting Table: 33
Beneficial Herbs: 35
Top 5 Benefits of Raised Bed Gardening: 39
Top 5 Benefits of Container Gardening: 45
Square Foot Gardening: 50
Creating Good Compost: 53
    Compost Mixes: 54
    More on Composting: 58
Thanks From The Author 65

Introduction to Companion Planting Vegetables:

Some individuals may consider companion planting to be some kind of 'New Age' holistic fad; however as the good book says 'There is nothing new under the sun.'

Although the whole aspect of companion planting seems finally to have gathered some recognition; the fact is that it has been practiced for centuries – ever since man first picked up a shovel and decided to grow his own food rather than (or as well as), chase it around with a bow and arrow!

In fact companion planting could be seen as the very foundation stone upon which the whole organic or green movement is built; the reason for this is simple. If done properly, companion planting does away with the need for chemical fertilisers and bug sprays; produces the best, healthy crops; and is the most environmentally friendly way to produce your own fresh food as a consequence.

Not only can you save money by 'going green,' but by making use of the companion planting methods described in this book, you – and your children – can live healthier lives by cutting out the chemical fertilizers and pesticides, that are inevitably included in the daily diet of those individuals who couldn't care less about what they consume, or indeed how it has been grown.

So what is Companion Planting?
Companion planting is simply a form of polyculture, and when used intelligently along with gardening techniques such as Raised Bed Gardening, Square Foot Gardening, or Container Gardening for instance; then this method of sharing the mutual benefits of the individual plants, is capable of producing fantastic results.

In fact, companion planting is likened to putting together the perfect partnership; creating results in respect of larger, healthier crops that the individual plants could not produce.

The fact is that, just like we homo-sapiens; plants need good companions to thrive and flourish in their environment. Unlike us however, being rooted to the spot, they cannot choose their friends – we have to choose friends or companions for them!

How do we choose 'friends' that they will like, and get along with? Simple really. We take into account the strong points and needs of the individual plants, and then put them together – in fact the gardener takes on the role of match-maker!

I'll bet you never considered running a dating agency for vegetables before this – did you? Joking apart; the fact is that if the plants thrive – alongside the ideal companions that you have provided - then the harvest is bountiful – and everyone is happy.

The History of Companion Planting:

As was alluded to in the introduction, companion planting is nothing new; and in fact is fairly well documented. The Chinese for instance, have been using this method to protect and promote their rice crops for over 1,000 years.

By planting the mosquito fern as a companion for their rice crops, that hosts a special cyanobacterium that fixes nitrogen from the atmosphere. It also helps to block out the light so that competing weeds cannot prosper; the rice being planted only when it is tall enough to stick above the fern.

The native Indians of North America are widely accredited for pioneering the 'Three Sisters' technique of planting corn, beans and squash together. The corn would act as a trellis for the beans, which in turn laid down nitrogen that benefited the corn and the squash.

Sunflowers could also be grown, usually a short distance away from the three sisters to act help draw away aphids.

Companion planting in fact, although ancient in origin, has grown up alongside the whole Organic Farming movement. With the emphasis on healthier foods, organically grown; this holistic approach to growing vegetables has taken on a whole new importance for the modern, environmentally aware grower.

Planting Zones:

There are a number of things to consider before you plan out your latest vegetable gardening project, and not the least of these by any measure, is the plant hardiness zones where you may or may not plant (with any degree of success) certain plant species.

Fundamentally a good rule of thumb when it comes to planting in your area, is to check out with other keen local gardeners just what they are growing. Get to know your neighbours – if you have not already done so – and glean all the local knowledge that you can.

With that in mind, consult the planting zone charts below this piece and plan out your garden accordingly.

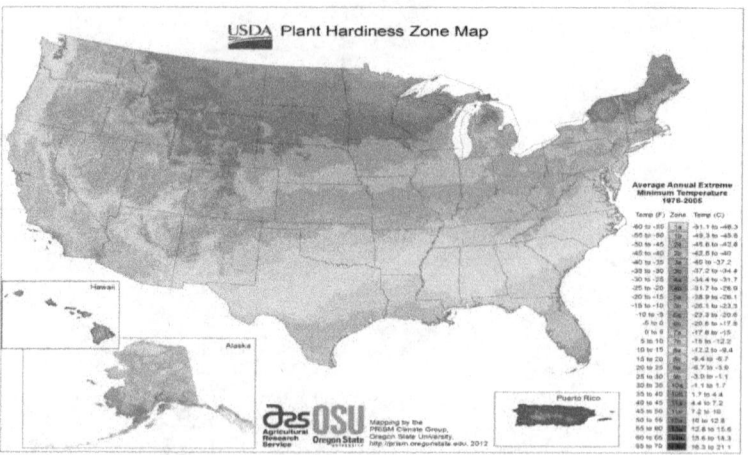

Average Annual Extreme Minimum Temperature 1976-2005

Temp (F)	Zone	Temp (C)
-60 to -55	1a	-51.1 to -48.3
-55 to -50	1b	-48.3 to -45.6
-50 to -45	2a	-45.6 to -42.8
-45 to -40	2b	-42.8 to -40
-40 to -35	3a	-40 to -37.2
-35 to -30	3b	-37.2 to -34.4
-30 to -25	4a	-34.4 to -31.7
-25 to -20	4b	-31.7 to -28.9
-20 to -15	5a	-28.9 to -26.1
-15 to -10	5b	-26.1 to -23.3
-10 to -5	6a	-23.3 to -20.6
-5 to 0	6b	-20.6 to -17.8
0 to 5	7a	-17.8 to -15
5 to 10	7b	-15 to -12.2
10 to 15	8a	-12.2 to -9.4
15 to 20	8b	-9.4 to -6.7
20 to 25	9a	-6.7 to -3.9
25 to 30	9b	-3.9 to -1.1
30 to 35	10a	-1.1 to 1.7
35 to 40	10b	1.7 to 4.4
40 to 45	11a	4.4 to 7.2
45 to 50	11b	7.2 to 10
50 to 55	12a	10 to 12.8
55 to 60	12b	12.8 to 15.6
60 to 65	13a	15.6 to 18.3
65 to 70	13b	18.3 to 21.1

UK Planting Zones:

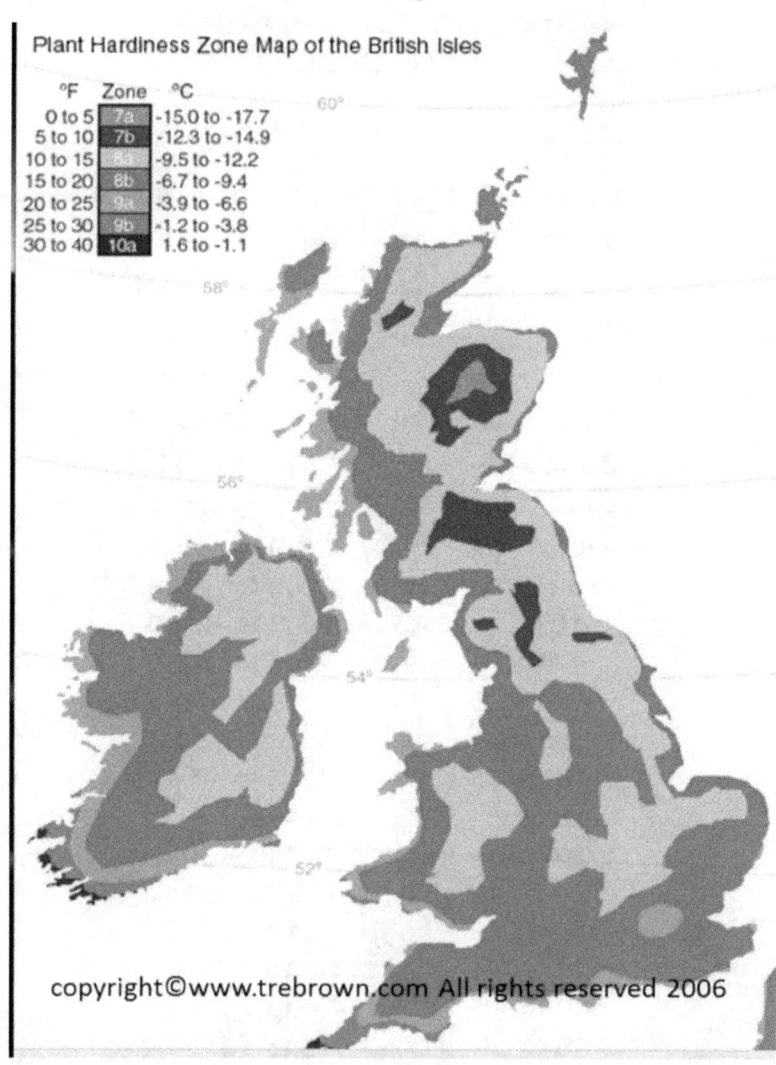

When buying seeds or plants then consult the seller or instructions on the packets to ascertain the correct plant according to the planting zone you are located in.

5 Good Reasons For Companion Planting:

There are many reasons that can be cited to promote the idea of companion planting, from environmental to personal. Here are just five of the most powerful reasons in my opinion.

1. Environmental:
Protecting the environment is a hugely important issue these days, and rightly so. If more people got themselves involved with the principles behind organic and companion gardening, then we would not be polluting both our bodies and the land, with chemical fertilizers or poisonous insecticides to the extent that we are.
This does not just involve ourselves, but has ramifications for generations to come.

Millions of tons of waste go into landfills every year, which in fact could easily be recycled – to our own benefit! Composting as a part of growing your own vegetables and becoming more environmentally aware, is one way to help balance this wastage.

It can be correctly stated that companion planting, when done in concert with other organic growing methods is good for our bodies and good for the environment – a win-win situation really.

2. Productivity
The main principle behind companion planting is the fact that when certain plants are grown together, then they benefit from one another, or at least the different plants can be grown together because they have different needs. This means that they are not competing for the same nutrients, or even atmospheric conditions.

With this being the case, then it also means that you can have a greater volume of plants in the same growing area, as they can be grown closer together without it being detrimental in any way – in fact if done correctly they will actually benefit from this closeness.

3. Easy maintenance:
The reason that companion planting generally means easier maintenance, may not at first be recognized. However the fact is that if the plants are chosen properly it means that they are planted closer together; meaning less of an area to cover when maintaining or harvesting your vegetables. This is especially relevant in a raised bed situation, where the area you have to cover is limited to the confines of the raised bed.

In this situation you have a 'double score' so to speak; as a raised bed garden is not so prone to weeds anyway, this coupled with correct companion planting, where the sunshine and nutrients are denied to weeds; leads to a situation where you are able maximise your efforts and get better results.

4. Natural insect control:
One of the big pluses for the companion planter is the fact that fewer insect problems occur, if the plants accompanying their neighbours are correctly chosen. For instance, if onions or leeks are planted alongside carrots, then problems with the dreaded carrot fly are less of an issue as the smell of the onions detracts the fly from the carrots.

Marigolds planted alongside your tomatoes will attract hover flies, which will protect them against aphids.
More examples to follow!

5. Less need for fertilizer
Again, if done correctly using organic methods of growing your vegetables, then there will be little if any need for artificial or chemical fertilizer.

The reason is two-fold. Firstly good organic compost in your growing area means that fertilizer should not be needed unless you are perhaps aiming to grow 'super crops.'

Secondly; if the plants are rotated properly, then the needs of one plant may in fact be supplied by the waste or productivity of another. For instance legumes like peas and beans are able to draw nitrogen from the atmosphere and deposit it into the ground. This benefits a multitude of other plants that flourish in a nitrogen-rich soil.
More of this 'fertile partnership' in later chapters.

The influence of Allelopathy:

Firstly you may be forgiven for saying to yourself "What the heck is Allelopathy?" It is not after all the kind of word that comes up in every day conversation!

However there is a fairly simple explanation. Allelopathy is in fact a process by which an organism produces bio chemical's that are beneficial to other organisms, for their growth or development.

These bio chemicals are called allelochemicals and can be either beneficial (positive Allelopathy) or detrimental (negative Allelopathy) to the target organisms – i.e. your vegetables.
In fact even the detrimental effects of plants can play an important part in any natural defence program against herbivores for instance, as they discourage grazing animals from eating your crops.

Allelopathy is characteristic of certain plants, bacteria, algae, coral, and fungi; and Allelopathic interaction between the species plays an important part in the success of many plant species.

Resource competition also plays a part in Allelopathy, as the various plants compete for the elements (water, light, or nutrition) that is required for their survival. Although not strictly speaking negative Allelopathy, this plays a part when deciding which plants to choose as companions between the species.

Allelopathy is playing an important part in researching different environmentally friendly ways of controlling weeds, or making crops more productive; without so much dependence on chemical fertilizers or insecticides.

Again, this is nothing new, and in fact as early as 300B.C. Theophrastus noted the inhibitory effects of pigweed on alfalfa crops; while in 1st century China 267 plants were recognised as having pesticidal properties that could be beneficial to other plants.

Peas and beans add much needed nitrogen that will benefit many plant species

Why Plants Grow Well Together:

To be a little more accurate here we have to look at what we mean by 'grow well together' in other words, in what way are they beneficial to each other's growth pattern. There are in fact three main ways that this can be so, and they are:

1. Nutritional

2. Protection

3. Decoy/Attractant

Nutrition:
In the first instance, nutrition is perhaps the first thing that springs to mind when it comes to advantageous companion planting; and indeed nutrition is of paramount importance in most cases.

Beans and peas, as in all legumes, draw in nitrogen and fix it into the soil. This in turn can provide the nutrients for corn for instance; which in turn can act as stalks for the beans.

If squash is planted around the stems then this will benefit from the nitrogen, and in turn cover the ground with their broad leaves, restricting the growth of weeds and other competitors for the nutrients. This is the typical 'three sisters' approach to companion planting.

Another good example is the 'square foot' gardening approach. This is especially applicable to raised bed gardening, and is a simple rotational method of growing crops in a confined space (16 square feet), that are beneficial to each neighbour, and so produce good vegetables without the need for fertilizers.

Protection:
However there are the issues of protection against insect or herbivore predation to consider, and this goes hand in hand in many cases with the 'decoy' aspect of companion planting.

Even protection against inclement weather plays a part in companion planting. For instance some plants prefer the shade, and so can grow under the shade provided by tall plants like Tomatoes. This can also provide protection against high winds or other weather conditions, that may be detrimental to some fruit or vegetable species.

Decoy/Attractant:
Certain plants are often used as either decoys to lure potential destructive insects away from vegetables; or indeed they can be used to attract beneficial insects like pollinating bees.

Insects can be controlled either by using the natural insect repellent abilities of some plants to scare the insects away; or by using the natural attraction of some plants to insects like aphids for instance; in order to encourage the aphids to attack this plant rather than the one you are promoting.

Marigolds for instance attract the hoverfly, who's larvae eat aphids from carrots or tomatoes.
Hosta's are often planted next to the vegetable patch to act as an attractant for the slugs, which seem to love the poor Hosta above everything else!

Nasturtiums are a classic example of this, and they are widely used to draw away aphids and other destructive pests. For this reason Hosta's and Nasturtiums are often referred to as sacrificial or Martyr plants, as they suffer in order to protect others.

These will be cover fuller in the examples below this article, where plants that grow well together, will be listed alongside the reasons why this is the case.

It is generally accepted amongst organic growers that planting masses of the same vegetable in long rows or concentrations is a bad idea. This is because by doing so you are attracting the predators of that one species from miles around – a bit like hanging a sign up and saying 'come and get me!'

Best practice is to intersperse your crops with herbs and/or flowers that protect your crop by disguising the smells and sights that attract the insects.

Plants That Grow Well Together:

Here is a list of plants that grow well together, with a brief explanation of just why this is the case. Although this list is not by any means an exhaustive list in itself; it only takes a little imagination to bring different species together, when you have the most basic gardening skills; and the knowledge that is contained in these notes to guide you.

Asparagus:
Best companions include: Tomato, parsley and Basil; and French marigold planted alongside will deter beetles. If on its own or just with Tomato plants, then Comfrey can be planted around as a good source of nitrogen for both plants.

Beans:
Companions include; Beetroot, cabbage, celery, carrot, cucumber, corn, squash, pea's, potatoes, radish, strawberry. Beans produce (draw from the air) nitrogen that is beneficial to the other plants
Nasturtium and rosemary can deter bean Beatles, while Marigolds can deter Mexican bean Beatles.

Cabbage Family:
Companions include; cucumber, potato, onion, spinach, celery.
Chamomile and garlic can be grown to improve growth and flavour.

Marigolds and Nasturtium can be grown alongside to act as decoy for butterfly's and aphid pests. While mint, rosemary and sage will also deter cabbage moth and ants – as well as improve flavour.

Marigolds planted next to carrots attract hover flies, who's larvae in turn eat aphids. The smell of the marigold flowers also confuse the carrot fly

Carrots:
Good companions include beans, peas, onions, lettuce, tomato, and radish.
Including chives in the area will improve flavour and growth, while onions or leeks will distract the carrot fly by masking the scent of the carrots; as will sage or rosemary.

Celery:
Bean, tomato and cabbage family make good companions for celery.
Nasturtium, chives and garlic deters aphids and other bugs.

Corn:
Good companions are Potato, pumpkin, squash, tomato and cucumber.
French marigold deters beetles and attracts aphids from tomatoes.

Cucumber:
Good companions include, cabbage, beans, cucumber, radish, tomato.
Marigold and Nasturtium are good for attracting to themselves, aphids and beetles. Oregano is a good all round pest deterrent.

Lettuce:
Carrot, beet, onion, and strawberry are all good companions for Lettuce.
Chives and garlic discourage aphids.

Melon:
Companions include pumpkin, radish, corn, and squash. Marigold and Nasturtium deters bugs and beetles, as does oregano.

Onions:
Good Companions include the cabbage family, beet, tomato, pepper, strawberry, peas, and chard.
Chamomile and summer savoury helps improve growth and flavour. Pigweed brings up nutrients from the subsoil, and improves conditions for the onions.

Parsley:
Good companions include asparagus, tomato and corn.

Parsnip:
Grows well alongside bush bean, onion, garlic, pepper, potato and squash.

Peas:
Good companions include beans, carrot, corn and radish. Chives and onions help deter aphids, as does nasturtium.

Planting mint is known to improve the health and flavour of peas.

Peppers:
Tomato, eggplant, carrot and onion are known to be good companions for peppers.

Potatoes:
Good companions include, bean, cabbage, squash and peas. Marigold makes a good general deterrent for beetles, while horseradish planted around the potato patch gives a good overall insect protection.

Pumpkin:
Melon eggplant and corn make good companions for pumpkin.
Oregano and Marigold give a good all round insect protection.

Radish:
Companions are carrot, cucumber, bean, pea, melon. Nasturtium planted around is generally accepted to improve growth and flavour.

Squash:
Companions include melon, pumpkin, and tomato; while nasturtium and marigold; along with oregano, helps protect against bugs and beetles.

Strawberry:
Good companions include bean, lettuce, onion and spinach. Planting thyme around the border deters worms, while borage strengthens general resistance to disease.

Tomatoes:
Good companion plants for tomatoes include; celery, cucumber, asparagus, parsley, pepper and carrot.
Basil and dwarf marigold deter flies and aphids; mint can improve health and all round flavour.

These are some examples from popular vegetable types, and offer a guide as to what to consider for your companion garden.
Next chapter takes a brief look at what plants do not grow well together for any number of reasons.

Plants That Do Not Grow Well Together:

There are a few reasons why some plants should not be grown alongside others if you are considering the organic method of growing your vegetables.

I mention particularly organic, because the general idea behind companion planting is to avoid the use of chemical pesticides and fertilizers whenever possible.

Some plants should not be grown together simply because they both attract the same pests or other predators, others because they make the same demands on the soil, leading to them both producing a poor harvest. Some plants grown close together may produce a damp environment that leads to fungal or other infection.

Here are some plants to avoid if possible when considering a companion for your veggies.

Beans:
Should not be grown in the same vicinity of garlic, shallot or onions, as they tend to stunt the growth of the beans.

Beets:
Should not be grown along with pole beans, as they stunt each other's growth.

Cabbage:
Is generally thought not to do well near tomatoes, mainly because the tomato plant can shade the cabbage. Avoid planting near radishes, or lettuce as they do not grow well together.

Carrots:
Avoid planting near dill as this can stunt growth. Dill and carrots both belong in the Umbelliferae family, and if allowed to flower it will cross-pollinate with the carrots.

Corn:
Avoid planting corn and tomatoes together, as they both attract the same tomato fruit-worm.

Cucumber:
Sage should be avoided near cucumber, as it generally injurious to the cucumber plant.

Kohlrabi:
Do not grow alongside pole beans, peppers, strawberry or tomatoes.

Leeks:
Avoid planting leeks near legumes. (peas, beans, peanuts or alfalfa).

Lettuce:

Does not prosper well beside cabbage, as the cabbage stunts growth and reduces the flavour of lettuce.

Peas:
Onions and garlic stunt the growth of peas.

Potatoes:
Tomatoes and potatoes should not be planted together as they attract the same blight.

Radish:
Avoid planting hyssop near radishes.

Quick Reference Companion Planting Table:

VEGETABLES	GOOD COMPANION	BAD COMPANION
Asparagus	tomato, parsley, basil	onion, garlic, potato
Beans	beetroot, cabbage, celery, carrot, cucumber, corn, squash, pea's, potatoes, radish	garlic, shallot or onions
Beets	broccoli, brussels sprouts, bush beans, cabbage, cauliflower	charlock, field mustard, pole beans
Cabbage	cucumber, potato, onion, spinach, celery.	Strawberries, tomato, lettuce
Carrots	beans, peas, onions, leeks, lettuce, tomato, and radish	dill
Celery	bean, tomato and cabbage family	corn, Irish potato and aster flowers
Corn	potato, pumpkin, squash, tomato, cucumber	tomatoes
Cucumber	cabbage, beans, cucumber, radish,	late potatoes

	tomato	
Eggplant	beans, peas, spinach, tarragon, thyme	potatoes, tomatoes, peppers
Garlic	cabbage, cane fruits, fruit trees, tomatoes	peas, beans
Leeks	carrots, celery, onions	all legumes
Lettuce	carrot, beet, onion, parsnip, strawberry	cabbage family
Melon	pumpkin, radish, corn, and squash	potatoes
Onions	cabbage family, beet, tomato, pepper, strawberry, peas, and chard	beans, peas
Parsley	asparagus, carrot, tomato and corn	mint
Peas	beans, carrot, corn and radish	garlic leeks, onions, shallots
Peppers	tomato, eggplant, carrot and onion	fennel, kohlrabi
Potatoes	bean, cabbage, squash and peas	apples, cherries, cucumbers, pumpkins, sunflowers, tomatoes
Pumpkin	melon eggplant	potato, raspberry

	and corn	
Radish	carrot, cucumber, bean, pea, melon	hyssop
Squash	melon, pumpkin, tomato, beans, cucumber, onion	potato, tomato
Strawberry	bean, lettuce, onion and spinach	cabbage, broccoli, brussels sprouts
Tomatoes	celery, cucumber, asparagus, parsley, pepper and carrot	fennel, kohlrabi, potatoes, beetroot, peas

Beneficial Herbs:

There are many herbs that can be extremely beneficial for your companion planting. Indeed the herbs themselves can lend that extra dimension to your vegetable garden, that will complement your vegetables – and improve your cooking!

Here is a list of some popular herbs along with the benefits they may have to certain plants.

Anise:
Anise is known to benefit beans and coriander plants.

Basil:

This is known to benefit asparagus, beans, cabbage and especially tomatoes.

It can be beneficial also as a 'sacrificial' plant in that it's soft leaves tend to attract butterflies and boring insects.

Caraway:

This is an ideal herb for breaking down and conditioning poor soils. It also attracts the attention of wasps and other harmful insects, making it a good 'sacrificial' herb. Also known to benefit strawberries and peas.

Chives:

An ideal companion for carrots, as it confuses the carrot fly. Also good around peppers, potato, rhubarb, squash or tomato plants, as it deters insects – particularly aphids.

Fennel:

This makes a **poor** companion plant for just about anything – avoid planting near other plants.

Lavender:

A good companion plant for many species as it's aromatic flowers attract many beneficial, pollinating insects to the garden.

It will also deter fleas, ticks and even mice!

Mint:

This is another all-round beneficial companion for many plant species; and in particular, peas, cabbage and tomatoes.

Mint is known also to deter insects, and even mice from your plants.

Parsley:
Asparagus is known to benefit particularly well, when grown alongside parsley; but carrots, cor, sweet peppers are also good companions.

Avoid planting near mint or lettuce.

Peppermint:
A good companion as it attracts beneficial insects and repels ants, aphids and cabbage fly.

Rosemary:
Beans, broccoli, cabbage, carrots and hot peppers all benefit from being planted alongside rosemary.

Planting carrots and pumpkins nearby is not advised as rosemary makes a poor companion for them.

Thyme:
Many plants such as cabbage, eggplant, potatoes and strawberries will benefit from planting thyme nearby; as it attracts many beneficial insects to the garden including honey bees.

It is also accredited with chasing off tomato hornworm, cabbage worms and flea beetles.

Top 5 Benefits of Raised Bed Gardening:

You may well ask why an article on container gardening, is included in this piece on companion planting? The answer is simple – they both go pretty much hand-in-hand, and have many mutual benefits in the whole field of organic or sustainable gardening.

Not everyone unfortunately, has the space needed to build a raised bed, and if that is the case then maybe the next chapter on container gardening may be off more interest. However please do not discount raised beds on this account – for many of the techniques are in fact interchangeable, and beneficial for better production.

1: Diversification:
With the concept of companion gardening in mind, diversification is a particularly relevant plus, when it comes to the idea of a raised bed garden. A raised bed allows for a more accurate method of planning your planting regime; particularly if you are following the 'square foot' method of gardening.

Crop rotation is particularly easy and effective with a raised bed, as everything is within hands reach. For many people the concept of a smaller growing area compared to say, a traditional garden plot; is much easier to get a grasp off and so work effectively.

For beneficial planting a raised bed is particularly simple, especially when considering herbs as the beneficial plants. In fact the close proximity of plants in a raised bed situation, actually calls out for a knowledge of companion planting, if the gardener is to avoid planting species that are not beneficial at all to one another.

2: Ease of operation:
There is no doubt at all that a raised bed, once built and established, is far easier to operate than a traditional vegetable plot.
The soil is fresh, and therefore mainly free from weeds for the first season at any rate. When weeds do come through, they are easy to manage because the soil is lighter, and the height of the bed itself makes it easier to manage.

General maintenance of the vegetables, as well as harvesting is easier for the same reason as above. The bed itself (usually 12-18" high) makes it much less of a back-breaking task when it comes to general servicing of your plot.

For the disabled or otherwise infirm, a raised bed system can be a real blessing as it allows access even from a wheelchair – provided the area around it has been kept clear, and any space between beds is built in to allow for the width of a wheelchair.

As beds are usually only 3 feet wide, this allows a user to reach into the center from both sides.
Building a raised bed with an edge of around 6 inches, is a good idea as it gives an immediate platform on which to lay tools, or sit on, or even put you glass on wine on!
Oh, and I almost forgot to mention – no more back-breaking double digging!

3: Pest 'free'
Ok, while not exactly pest free, raised beds are without doubt easier to keep pests away from. Quite apart from the companion planting methods described above; the simple fact is that a raised bed is easier to erect a simple frame for netting around, or indeed covering with clear polythene to form a mini-green house. This can be used to bring on plants that prefer warmer climates, and can also deter flying insects.

The fact that your vegetables are raised off the ground, also means that they are not so prone to crawling critters, determined to snack on your precious veg.

What about slugs? Simple, tack some copper tape around the outside edge of the frame, and the slugs will no cross over to wreak their usual devastation. This is because slug-slime has a chemical reaction with the copper that means slugs cannot cross over it.

Even burrowing critters such as rats, mice or gophers; can be stopped by simply putting wire mesh on the base of the raised bed before it is filled in, thus preventing them from burrowing upwards to munch on your veggies.

4: More productive
A raised bed is generally far more productive than a traditional vegetable plot, for a number of reasons. The first is that the soil in a raised bed has been specially chosen by yourself; and should be 80% good well-rotted organic material, to 20% actual good quality garden soil.

This means that you are not trying to plant in poor quality, clay-filled soil that is perhaps poorly drained and full of weeds that are competing for the limited nutrients available.

The fact that coupling companion planting techniques, along with the ability to plant much closer together; means that you will produce a much higher yield, than you would in a traditional garden layout.
More time spent harvesting and less time spent pulling out weeds, must be a great result for any gardener.

5: Longer growing season
Because a raised bed is by definition, raised out of the ground; it warms up quicker in the early spring and catches the last rays ant the end of the season. The result of this, depending on where you live, can easily add another month on to the growing season; as you can plant much earlier, and continue harvesting your crops until later in the season.

This results in your plants generally being more productive, and you extending your gardening season! This means also that your whole growing regime can become much more cost-effective as your overall growing time is extended.

Other things to consider:
One of the important things to consider when you are building your raised bed, is the growing medium itself. I deliberately describe it as 'growing medium' because it is not garden soil. The mixture of 80/20 above is an indication that the infill must be a mix of compost and soil, and not soil alone.

The reason for this is two-fold. First of all, you will be far more productive with your efforts, if you include a properly balanced mix of organic material into your raised bed. Secondly, if you just fill in your raised bed with soil alone, then it will turn into a solid mass within your frame-work, and as a result will (understandably) become less productive and more labour intensive to maintain.

Top 5 Benefits of Container Gardening:

To begin with, please do not think that container gardening is the 'poor mans raised bed,' as some would have it. The fact is that even a raised bed, is a type of container garden if you think about it. All your planting is in effect 'contained' within the boundaries of the raised bed framework after all. However, without meaning to be facetious – lets quickly move on to the benefits of container gardening.

1: It's mobile!

Unlike a raised bed or a traditional garden; a garden built around the idea of containers has the advantage of mobility. This means that you can move around you containers to get best advantage of the sunlight, or indeed the shade. When pursuing the ideals of companion gardening; this is particularly effective as you can move around say pots of herbs, in order to protect various vegetable species from insect attack.

If you use smaller containers that can easily be shifted, you can move them around a patio or decking area, for purely aesthetic reasons; for instance flowering chives make a particularly beautiful backdrop, As does lavender or many other scented herbs.

2: Limitless containers
When it comes to the things you can use for your containers, the choices are virtually limitless; and restricted only to your imagination and the overall effect you wish to achieve. Everything from costly ornamental pots, to garden pails and even paint tins can be used for growing in containers – just be sure there is no residue of the previous occupant hanging around inside!

Using containers can be seen as a viable way to recycle old material and prevent it rotting in a landfill somewhere. Old wheelbarrows make good containers for growing vegetables, as do old tyres piled up, lined and filled with compost. Not moveable like the smaller pots – but very effective nevertheless (Great for growing potatoes in a stack!)

3: Insect repellent

In the same way as raised beds are more insect repellent because they sit off the ground; containers have a similar advantage over ground grown veg, in that they can be raised off the ground and so not so vulnerable to creeping insect attack.

You can also paint around the pot rim with copper paint; this will keep the slugs at bay. Strawberries grown in this way can be particularly effective as they are free from the predations of slugs; and they are limited as to their spreading abilities.

4: Space preserving
Especially for those who are not fortunate enough to have a raised bed or a traditional garden area; container gardening is really suited to the gardener who has a limited space to grow in.
Even with a small patio or balcony; indeed within the confines of the house itself, it is possible to grow a range of fruit and vegetables in pots for very little cost.

The main thing to consider is the size (and position) of the pot compared to the plant's needs. Whilst a tomato plant needs a two gallon pail at least to grow effectively; a pepper plant can be grown in a simple plant-pot and produce a good harvest of hot peppers.

5: Its good for you!

Ok, that's a very broad statement admittedly; however the fact is that growing vegetables, whether in raised beds or containers is beneficial in a number of ways for the grower. There is the environmental issues to take into consideration, inasmuch as you are reducing your needs for plastic-wrapped vegetables from the store – thereby saving the planet from your pollution.

The health issues are self-explanatory in that you are producing your own food, so should know exactly what goes into it – unlike the produce in the stores.

The fact that you are picking the food from your own premises, instead of from a store where it has been stocked after maybe thousands of miles in transportation; means that you are reducing your own 'carbon footprint' to zero.

Finally it has to be recognised even by the most negative sceptic, that gardening in general has a beneficial outcome, in that it is good for the purposes of relaxation. What better place to get away from the hassles that constantly bombard the mind; than by tending your garden – container or otherwise.

****

There is another aspect of container garden that should not be overlooked, and that is the versatility of container gardening; and in particular how it can be used alongside raised bed or conventional gardening in order to get the best results from each discipline.

By this I mean that you can take your companion planting knowledge and use it by planting say marigolds or mint in containers, and then placing them alongside the plants that will benefit from them.

For instance you could place pots with onions or shallots in amongst your carrot patch to save them from the carrot fly. Or perhaps place pots with French marigolds under your tomato plants to save them from voracious greenfly.

Square Foot Gardening:

'Square foot gardening' is a phrase accredited to Mel Bartholomew who popularised the idea back in the 1980's with a TV gardening program in the USA.

Along with the Raised Bed Gardening concept however, it is actually an adaptation of a growing or planting technique that has been known to our fore-fathers for generations – even millennia!

These days it is particularly relevant for people with the desire to grow their own vegetables, even though they may have limited space in which to do so.

The typical SFG is a square frame 6 inches high and forming a square 4 feet by 4 feet = 16 square feet. It is usually formed with lumber, but in fact can be made with any suitably robust material that you may have to hand including cinder blocks or bricks.

This is a planting system 'rooted' in the concept of companion planting, as the close proximity of plants that have been chosen for their 'good companion' status, helps to both disguise and benefit, nutritionally and in other ways, their immediate neighbours.

Plants are chosen according to their benefits to neighbours, and of course to climatic and other considerations. The picture below is a typical SFG layout showing the plants and numbers planted.

South Facing

RADISH (16)	RADISH (16)	BEET (9)	BEET (9)
CARROTS (16)	CARROTS (16)	CUCUMBER (2)	CUCUMBER (2)
PEPPER (1)	PEPPER (1)	POTATO (1)	POTATO (1)
CORN (3)	CORN (3)	PEAS (8)	PEAS (8)

Although good companion planting is essential to get the best out of a SFG, the driving force is actually the growing medium which allows for little or no added nutrients during the growing and maturing process.

A mixture of compost, water retainer and peat is used to great effect along with proper companions, to guarantee good crops with minimum effort on the part of the grower.

In the next section on composting in general, there will be included some 'recipes' for your SFG or indeed other growing methods including Raised Bed and Container Planting.

If you are interested in the concepts of Raised Bed or Square Foot gardening, then you will find lots more detailed information on these subjects by clicking on the links at the beginning of this book.

Creating Good Compost:

(Includes A Selection of Material Taken From <u>Authors Book On SFG</u>)

When it comes to making a good organic compost, there is the quick way and the longer way. If you are about to build your raised bed garden, or indeed fill in your pots already – then no doubt you will be looking for the quick way!

Quick organic compost mix:
First of all you need some well-rotted manure, preferably horse or chicken, then mix that with a good quality topsoil, mixed with general garden compost from the local garden center. I generally find that a mix of around 60% compost, 20% well-rotted manure and 20% soil makes for a good all-round growing medium.

This mixture may of course be changed, for instance if you wish to grow champion leeks, then heavier manure content should be considered.

More details on compost mixes to follow in later chapters.

Compost Mixes:

There are many different mixes of compost that will suit certain plants more than others, and this is great if you are specializing in a specific area like growing giant pumpkins!

However if you have a source of well-rotted manure, then this is ideal for crops such as tomatoes, beans, peas, leeks - in fact just about anything, as rotted manure is a great source of nitrogen which every plant needs in different quantities.

There are certain plants that also make valuable additions to the compost heap such as nettles, which speed up decomposition and add valuable nitrogen, or comfrey, which is a terrific source of potash (potassium) and has a high carbon to nitrogen ratio – which is ideal for most plants and perfect for tomatoes, fruit and berries.

If you are working a homestead or hobby farm then you almost certainly have access to chicken manure! This is very rich in nitrogen and a fantastic addition to your compost.

Be sure though to let it rot for at least 1 year to kill off any parasites or eggs that may be in it; also it needs this time to 'mellow' otherwise it is too strong in nitrogen for most plants to tolerate.

When using manure of any kind you have the option to add it to your composting heap while they are both still in the process of decomposing; or you may add the fully decomposed manure directly to your SFG as part of the mix.

When has manure decomposed enough to use?
You will know when the manure has finished decomposing when it has a deep 'earthy' smell – not smelling of dung; and the material itself should be relatively dry and crumbly when handled.

If it still smells of dung then it has not finished decomposing and should be left for a further few weeks or even months.

Here is a chart to show just what the different animal dungs 'bring to the table' with regard to percentage values of nutrients.

	NITROGEN	PHOSPHORUS	POTASH
Average farmyard manure	0.64	0.23	0.32
Pure pig dung	0.48	0.58	0.36
Pure cow dung	0.44	0.29	0.49

Horse Manure	0.49	0.29	0.58
Deep litter on straw	0.80	0.55	0.48
Fresh Poultry Dung	1.66	0.91	0.45
Pigeon Dung	5.84	2.10	1.77

A good composting mix for raised beds and containers particularly, has to be light and airy; this will promote excellent growth and be easy to maintain with regard to weed-pulling and other general gardening tasks.

Apart from the mixes already mentioned, here are some mixes for my SFG and Raised Beds that I have had great success with.

Mix 1: 60% compost, 20% washed sand, 20% peat moss.

Mix 2: 40% compost, 20% fish meal, 30% coconut coir and 10% good topsoil.

Mix 3: 50% compost, 20% vermiculite (or perlite), 30% peat moss.

Mix 4: 50% compost, 30% peat moss, 20% quality topsoil.

Mix 5: 40% compost, 40% peat moss, 20% vermiculite.

More on Composting:

As mentioned, Compost takes time to mature, that is the hard facts of decomposition I'm afraid. However any serious gardener is always looking ahead at least one or two seasons, and preparing their growing plans accordingly.

To create your own compost; you should ideally have a composting bin, or a box arrangement that has a lid; this will keep away vermin, and prevent the rain from cooling down the compost.

A simple wooden structure made from recycled pallets will often make a very effective composting bin. Be sure that the opening is wide enough to allow for turning the contents with a garden fork occasionally to improve the composting process.

The materials for good compost should be layered in order to get the best effect, as in the picture below. This neat layering will of course be upset after the first turning over; however it gives the whole composting process a good start and ensures a proper mix of materials.

Compost Ingredients:

Carbon (Dried Matter): Dried leaves, straw, wood chips, grass, small twigs.

Nitrogen (fresh matter): Vegetable scraps, lawn clippings, weeds, manure.

Soil: The addition of good soil adds minerals and micro-organisms to the compost, thereby stimulating aerobic composition.

This layering process – including watering well between layers - generates significant heat which also kills disease organisms and weed seeds etc, in effect making it suitable for use in the garden. If there is a shortage of nitrogen then the whole process is lengthened. The job of the good compost maker is to see that this is not the case and provide suitable quantities of air, moisture and nitrogen to the mix.

With all this in mind a good composter should be constructed in such a way as to ensure good ventilation to the mix; as well as allow for turning the compost (for aeration).

Traditionally Nitrogen can be added to the mix by adding fresh dung as the nitrogen is in the urine; or by adding suitable plants such as nettles (without the roots) and grass clippings which are rich in nitrogen.

As different materials decay at different times, it is also advisable to have not just one composter, but three at least if you have the space for them. This way you can really take control over your composting efforts.

Material to consider for composting; can in theory be anything organic in nature, and includes such things as vegetable cuttings, tea bags, shredded paper, garden waste, grass cuttings, seaweed, comfrey leaves, kitchen waste, shrub cuttings, wood ash and fallen leaves.

If you have a good source of leaves available, then one of the simplest composters to make is perhaps the weld-mesh composter. Simply get some 2" weld-mesh cut from the roll so that it forms a tube about 18 - 24" across.

Cut so that there are wire ends that you can fold over, then bend the wire ends into itself where the end of the wire tube meets; so that it forms a permanent tube shape, then stand upright.

You should be left with a simple wire-mesh tube. This can then be filled with leaves to form a rich compost material.

If you make several of these tubes, they can even be arranged to form a kind of 'compost fence'- a great source of compost and a good talking point amongst the visitors!

Not everything organic is good for creating compost however, and material to leave out of the composter, include meat by-products, eggs or dairy products – unless you are considering **Bakashi Composting** which does in fact utilize these products very effectively.

Dog and cat dirt or litter, should never be put in the composter. Meat, bones or fish scraps should be kept out. Never put ashes from a coal fire into the composter, as this introduces sulphur to the mix.
Small amounts of wood ash is acceptable however as it introduces lime and potash, as well as magnesium and phosphoric acid, all of which are good for enriching the soil.

When adding or building up your compost, then it is a good idea to layer occasionally with some straw, garden soil, or fine twigs This all helps with the general aeration of the mix and the composting process.

Composting Materials Time-line:

Here is a short list of composting materials and the time taken to compost in ideal conditions.

Materials taking 6 months +
Kitchen vegetable trimmings (beware - stems and stalks take 2-3 years or more), annual weeds, fruit peel, lawn trimmings (no more than 15cm thick).

Material taking 1 – 2 years
Hedge clippings and prunings (except conifers and evergreens which will take more than 3 years to break down completely), paper and cardboard, autumn leaves.

Material taking 3 years +
Thick stalks and stems of plants, evergreens including holly or conifers, eggshells, sawdust & wood shavings, or thick layers of grass clippings.
Any other organic material that is large and bulky will naturally take longer to compost.

Another Option?
Finally, if you have no space to compost, or no time or whatever – consider your local authority! Many municipal authorities are composting as part of their environmental efforts, this is highly regulated and usually excellent quality – and it is often given away free or for very little cost!

If that option is not available or you would like to get started growing your vegetables immediately; then you can certainly go for store-bought, while your own composting efforts are a 'work in progress.'

Patience:
Something that can be in short supply for most people! It does however take patience to produce good compost, and usually a two year period will be required to get the best out of your composting efforts. The results however will show in the quality of your vegetables, and the general health of your garden.

Leaves and grass cuttings can take a particularly long time to fully rot down. How do you know if the material is well rotted? In general terms, well-rotted material should have a healthy earthy smell, and not smell like it is still rotting! It will be crumbly in your hand, and not be over wet and cloggy.

After all that effort, then you will also have the feel-good factor in knowing that you have done your bit for the environment – never to be underestimated!

Measuring volumes:
If you're buying bagged soil and making your own mix, here is an indication of what you may require. To use a 4' x 4' bed that is 12" high for the example; you first want to get

your volume. Remember that 1 cubic yard equals 27 cubic feet. And to get your bed volume multiply the width, length and height in feet.

4 x4 x 1 = 16 cubic feet. This is how many cubic feet of soil your bed will require. If you're buying 2 cubic foot bags then the bed will take 8 bags, if you're buying 1 cubic foot bags, then it will take around 16 bags.

A raised bed measuring 6 foot by 3 foot and 18 inches high for instance, would take 27 cubic feet of compost. A simple calculation will provide the volume you need for whatever size of raised bed you may have.

Thanks From The Author

Let me just finish by saying a **HUGE THANK YOU** for purchasing my book – it is very much appreciated.

If you have enjoyed it (and hopefully you have!) then I would be delighted if you could take the time to post a quick review on Amazon – you're honest opinion will be valued by myself and other potential readers.

If you would like more information on the aspects of Raised Bed Gardening as well as other highly effective gardening or Homesteading techniques, then please feel free to check out the following books

******

Relevant Books by Same Author

Raised Bed Gardening 5 Book Bundle
Square Foot Gardening
Square Foot Vs Raised Bed Gardening
Vegetable Gardening Basics
Organic Pest Control

Or simply check out my Authors Page for a selection of gardening books covering many different gardening disciplines.

http://amazon.com/author/jamesparis